CW01373362

THE PEOPLE'S OTHERWORLD

Also by Les A. Murray

The Ilex Tree (with Geoffrey Lehmann)
The Weatherboard Cathedral
Poems Against Economics
Lunch and Counter Lunch
Ethnic Radio
The Peasant Mandarin (selected prose)
The Boys Who Stole the Funeral
The Vernacular Republic: Poems 1961-1981

THE PEOPLE'S OTHERWORLD

Poems by Les A. Murray

ANGUS & ROBERTSON PUBLISHERS

Published with the assistance of the Literature Board of the
Australia Council.

ANGUS & ROBERTSON PUBLISHERS
London • Sydney • Melbourne

This book is copyright. Apart from any fair dealing for the
purposes of private study, research, criticism or review, as
permitted under the Copyright Act, no part may be reproduced
by any process without written permission. Inquiries should
be addressed to the publishers.

First published in Australia by Angus & Robertson Publishers in 1983
First published in the United Kingdom by Angus & Robertson (UK)
Ltd in 1983

Copyright © Les A. Murray 1983

National Library of Australia
Cataloguing-in-publication data.

Murray, Les A. (Leslie Allan), 1938- .
  The people's otherworld.
  ISBN 0 207 14639 X.
  I. Title.
A821'.3

Typeset in 10pt English Times by Graphicraft Typesetters Limited
Printed in Hong Kong

*To the glory of God
and in
memory of Anne, Steve,
Rosalind and Chris*

ACKNOWLEDGEMENTS

Poems in this book have been published in the *Age*, *Age Monthly Review*, *Artlook*, *Aspect*, *Bulletin*, *Cencrastus*, *Fiction Magazine*, *Helix*, *Independence*, *Island*, *Meanjin*, *Newcastle Herald*, *New Yorker*, *Occident*, *Persea International Review*, *Poetry Australia*, *PN Review*, *Quadrant*, *Quarto*, *The Review*, *Sydney Morning Herald*, *Threepenny Review* and *Times Literary Supplement,* and some have been broadcast by the Australian Broadcasting Commission and the British Broadcasting Corporation.

I am grateful to the Scottish Arts Council, the Library of Congress, the Association of American Poets and the Universities of Stirling, Copenhagen, Newcastle and New South Wales for hospitality and assistance extended to me during the years when these poems were being written.

CONTENTS

For a Jacobite Lady   1
The Craze Field of Dried Mud   2
The Grassfire Stanzas   4
Homage to the Launching Place   6
First Essay on Interest   8
The Fishermen at South Head   10
The Doorman   11
The Sydney Highrise Variations   12
    1. *Fuel stoppage on Gladesville road bridge in the year 1980*
    2. *View of Sydney, Australia, from Gladesville road bridge*
    3. *The flight from Manhattan*
    4. *The C19-20*
    5. *The recession of the Joneses*
Quintets for Robert Morley   17
The New Moreton Bay   19
Anthropomorphics   20
The Romantic Theme of Ruins   21
Bent Water in the Tasmanian Highlands   23
Equanimity   24
The Forest Hit by Modern Use   26
Shower   27
The Quality of Sprawl   28
Three Poems in Memory of My Mother   30
    Weights
    Midsummer Ice
    The Steel
Machine Portraits with Pendant Spaceman   37
The International Poetry Festivals Thing   41
Little Boy Impelling a Scooter   43
Self-Portrait from a Photograph   44
The Hypogeum   46
An Immortal   47
Second Essay on Interest: The Emu   48
A Retrospect of Humidity   50
Flowering Eucalypt in Autumn   51
The Chimes of Niegeschah   52
The Smell of Coal Smoke   54
The Mouthless Image of God in the Hunter-Colo Mountains   55
Time Travel   57
Exile Prolonged by Real Reasons   58
Three Interiors   60
Morse   62

Late Snow in Edinburgh 63
Art History: The Suburb of Surrealls 64
The Dialectic of Dreams 65
Satis Passio 67

For a Jacobite Lady

Proud heart, since the light of making lace
for an exiled prince died in your eyes
it is above two centuries.

Your Cause grew literary as it died;
it was Gothic in classicising times
and a wilder gothic extinguished it,

but you are there in the heat of it,
codes, glasses, the waiting on Versailles,
the sin of hope that eats the heart.

Your needle has left what it could trace:
your life's thread, in endless free returns,
making little subjoined worlds of grace.

That was monarchy. At its defeat
earth fell against heaven, and everyone
was exposed to glory in the street.

I write you this from the Land of Peace,
the Plain of Sports of the vision-poems;
your wars drove us here; we possess it now.

We are descendants. As was our one Prince.
Not over the water, but in the wine,
he is more assailed now, since more visible,

freed from the robes of any court.
Causes are our courts: they try our lives
and sentence us by mere report

as if to see both sides of death
truly, at once, in their due weight
were not reserved to the consummate.

The Craze Field of Dried Mud

These lagoons, these anabranches,
streets of the underworld.
Their water has become the trees that stand along them.

Below root-revetments, in the circles of the water's recession
the ravines seem thronged with a legacy of lily pads.
Earth curls and faintly glistens, scumbled painterly and peeling.

Palates of drought-stilled assonance,
they are cupped flakes of grit, crisps of bottom, dried meniscus
lifted at the edges.

Abstracts realised in slime. Shards of bubble, shrivelled viscose
of clay and stopped life:
the scales of the water snake have gone to grey on this channel.

— O —

Exfoliate bark of the rain tree, all the outer
plaques have a jostling average size.
It is a kind of fire, the invention of networks.

Water's return, however gradual (and it won't be)
however gentle (it won't be) would not re-lay all seamless
this basal membrane;
it has borne excess of clarity.

This is the lush sheet that overlay the first cities,
the mother-goddess towns, but underlay them first.
This they had for mortar.

Laminar, half detached, these cusps are primal tissue,
foreshadowings of leaf, pottery, palimpsest,
the Dead Lagoon Scrolls.

In this hollow season
everything is perhaps to be recapitulated,
hurriedly, approximately. It is a kind of fire.
Saturate calm is all sprung, in the mother country.

— O —

The lagoon-bed museums meanwhile have a dizzy stillness
that will reduce, with all the steps that are coming,
to meal, grist, morsels.
Dewfall and birds' feet have nipped, blind noons have nibbled
this mineral matzoh.

The warlike peace-talking young, pacing this dominion
in the beautiful flesh that outdoes their own creations
might read gnomic fragments:
> *corr   lux   Romant   irit*

or fragmentary texts:
> *who lose belief in God will not only believe*
> *in anything; they will bring blood offerings to it*

Bones, snags, seed capsules
intrinsic in the Martian central pan
are hidden, in the craze, under small pagoda eaves.

The Grassfire Stanzas

August, and black centres expand on the afternoon paddock.
Dilating on a match in widening margins, they lift
a splintering murmur; they fume out of used-up grass
that's been walked, since summer, into infinite swirled licks.

The man imposing spring here swats with his branch, controlling it;
only small things may come to a head, in this settlement pattern.

Fretted with small flame, the aspiring islands leave
odd plumes behind. Smuts shower up every thermal
to float down long stairs. Aggregate smoke attracts a kestrel.

Eruption of darkness from far down under roots
is the aspect of these cores, on the undulating farmland;
dense black is withered into web, inside a low singing;
it is dried and loosened, on the surface; it is made weak.

The green feed that shelters beneath its taller death yearly
is unharmed, under new loaf soot. Arriving hawks teeter
and plunge continually, working over the hopping outskirts.

The blackenings are balanced, on a gradient of dryness
in the almost-still air, between dying thinly away
and stripping the whole countryside. Joining, they never gain
more than they lose. They spread away from their high moments.

The man carries smoke wrapped in bark, and keeps applying it
starting new circles. He is burning the passive ocean
around his ark of buildings and his lifeboat water.

It wasn't this man, but it was man, sing the agile
exclamatory birds, who taught them this rapt hunting
(strike! in the updrafts, snap! of hardwood pods).
Humans found the fire here. It is inherent. They learn,
wave after wave of them, how to touch the country.

Sterilising reed distaffs, the fire edges onto a dam;
it circuits across a cow-track; new surf starts riding outward
and a nippy kestrel feeds from its foot, over cooling mergers.

It's the sun that is touched, and dies in expansion, mincing,
making the round dance, foretelling its future, driving
the frantic lives outwards. The sun that answers the bark tip
is discharged in many little songs, to forestall a symphony.

Cattle come, with stilted bounding calves, They look across the
ripple lines of heat, and shake their armed heads at them;
at random, then, they step over. Grazing smudged black country
they become the beasts of Tartarus. Wavering, moving out over
dung-smouldering ground still covered with its uncovering.

Homage to the Launching Place

Pleasure-craft of the sprung rhythms, bed,
                      kindest of quadrupeds,
you are also the unrocking boat
                      that moves on silence.

Straining hatchway into this world,
                      you sustain our collapses
above earth; guarantor of evolution,
                      you are our raised baseline.

Resisting gravity, for us and in us,
                      you form a planet-wide
unobtrusive discontinuous platform,
                      a layer: the mattressphere,

pretty nearly our highest common level
                      (tables may dispute it).

                      Muscles' sweatprinted solace,
godmother of butt-stubbing dreams,
                      you sublimate, Great Vehicle,
all our upright passions;

                      midwife of figuring, and design,
you moderate them wisely;
                      aiming solitude outwards, at action,
you sigh Think some more. Sleep on it ...

Solitude. Approaching rest
Time reveals her oscillation
                      and narrows into space;
                      there is time in that dilation:
                      Mansions. Defiles. Continents.
                      The living and the greatly living,

                      objects that take sides,
                      that aren't morally neutral

you accept my warm absence
                      there, as you will accept,
one day, my cooling presence.

                      I loved you from the first, bed,
doorway out of this world;
                      above your inner springs
I learned to dig my own.

                        Primly dressed, linen-collared one,
you look so still, for your speed,
                        shield that carries us to the fight
                        and bears us from it.

First Essay on Interest

Not usury, but interest. The cup slowed in mid-raise,
the short whistle, hum, the little forwards shift
mark our intake of that non-physical breath

which our lungs mimic sharply, to cancel the gap in pressure
left by our self vanishing into its own alert —
A blink returns us to self, that intimate demeanour

self-repairing as a bow-wave. What we have received
is the ordinary mail of the otherworld, wholly common,
not postmarked divine; no one refuses delivery,

not even the eagle, her face fixed at heavy Menace:
I have juices to sort the relevant from the irrelevant;
even her gaze may tilt left, askance, aloof, right,
fixing a still unknown. Delaying huge flight.

Interest. Mild and inherent with fire as oxygen,
it is a sporadic inhalation. We can live long days
under its surface, breathing material air

then something catches, is itself. Intent and special silence.
This is interest, that blinks our interests out
and alone permits their survival, by relieving

us of their gravity, for a timeless moment;
that centres where it points, and points to centering,
that centres us where it points, and reflects our centre.

It is a form of love. The everyday shines through it
and patches of time. But it does not mingle with these;
it wakens only for each trace in them of the Beloved.

And this breath of interest is non-rhythmical:
it is human to obey, humane to be wary of rhythm
as tainted by the rallies, as marching with the snare-drum.
The season of interest is not fixed in the calendar cycle;

it pulls towards acute dimensions. Death is its intimate.
When that Holland of cycles, the body, veers steeply downhill
interest retreats from the face; it ceases to instil
and fade, like breath; it becomes a vivid steady state

that registers every grass-blade seen on the way,
the long combed grain in the steps, free insects flying;
it stands aside from your panic, the wracked disarray;
it behaves as if it were the part of you not dying.

Affinity of interest with extremity
seems to distil to this polar disaffinity
that suggests the beloved is not death, but rather
what our death has hidden. Which may be this world.

The Fishermen at South Head

They have walked out as far as they can go on the prow of the continent,
on the undercut white sandstone, the bowsprits of the towering headland.
They project their long light canes
or raise them up to check and string, like quiet archers.
Between casts they hold them couched,
a finger on the line, two fingers on a cigarette, the reel cocked.

They watch the junction of smooth blue with far matt-shining blue,
the join where clouds enter,
or they watch the wind-shape of their nylon
bend like a sail's outline
south towards, a mile away, the city's floating gruel
of gull-blown effluent.

Sometimes they glance north, at the people on that calf-coloured edge
lower than theirs, where the suicides come by taxi
and stretchers are winched up
later, under raining lights
but mostly their eyes stay level with the land-and-ocean glitter.

Where they stand, atop the centuries
of strata, they don't look down much
but feel through their tackle the talus-eddying
and tidal detail of that huge simple pulse
in the rock and in their bones.

Through their horizontal poles they divine the creatures of ocean:
a touch, a dip, and a busy winding death gets started;
hands will turn for minutes, rapidly,
before, still opening its pitiful doors, the victim
dawns above the rim, and is hoisted in a flash above the suburbs
— or before the rod flips, to stand
trailing sworn-at gossamer.

On that highest dreadnought scarp, where the terracotta
waves of bungalows stop, suspended at sky,
the hunters stand apart.
They encourage one another, at a distance, not by talk

but by being there, by unhooking now and then
a twist of silver for the creel, by a vaguely mutual
zodiac of cars TV windcheaters.
Braced, casual normality. Anything unshared,
a harlequin mask, a painted wand flourished at the sun
would anger them. It is serious to be with humans.

The Doorman

The man applying rules to keep me out
knows if I have to deal with him the rules
apply to me. I am to be kept out.
Naive to think that he respects the rules;
he knows their purpose. Complicity is out:
if I were his sort I would know the rules.

His genes have seeped down a hundred centuries;
in a slave-ship's hold they pooled to form his eyes,
on a Sunday school mop they collected to a face
and they formed a skin in the dry air of a palace.
In stripes, in armour, in pinstripes, he stays the same man
and I know his sister, that right-thinking woman.

He is a craftsman, and these are his tools:
unyielding correctness, thin mouth, a nose for clout,
modulations of boredom (let the blusterers threaten).
He guards the status quo as he guards mankind's salvations
and those he protects need never learn the rules:
his contempt is reserved for those who are In, and Out.

The Sydney Highrise Variations

1. *Fuel stoppage on Gladesville road bridge in the year 1980*

So we're sitting over our sick beloved engine
atop a great building of the double century
on the summit that exhilarates cars, the concrete vault on its thousands
of tonnes of height, far above the tidal turnaround.

Gigantic pure form, all exterior, superbly uninhabited
or peopled only by transients at speed, the bridge
is massive outline.
                    It was inked in by scaffolding and workers.
Seen from itself, the arch
is an abstract hill, a roadway up-and-over without country,
from below, a ponderous grotto, all entrance and vast shade
framing blues and levels.

From a distance, the flyover on its vaulting drum
is a sketched stupendous ground burst, a bubble raising surface
or a rising heatless sun with inset horizons.
                                      Also it's a space probe,
a trajectory of strange fixed dusts, that were milled,
boxed with steel-rod mesh and fired, in dense stages,
from sandstone point to point. They docked at apogee.

It feels good. It feels right.
The joy of sitting high is in our judgement.
The marvellous brute-force effects of our century work.
They answer something in us. Anything in us.

2. *View of Sydney, Australia, from Gladesville road bridge*

There's that other great arch eastward, with its hanging highways;
the headlands and horizons of packed suburb, white among bisque-fired; odd
                                                                                                  smokes rising;
there's Warrang, the flooded valley, that is now the ship-chained Harbour,
recurrent everywhere, with its azure and its grains;
ramped parks, bricked containers,
verandas successive around walls,
and there's the central highrise, multi-storey, the twenty-year countdown,
the new city standing on its haze above the city.

                      Ingots of shear
                      affluence poles
                      bomb-drawing grid
                      of columnar profit
                      piecrust and scintillant
                      tunnels in the sky
                      high window printouts
                      repeat their lines
                      repeat their lines
                      credit conductors
                      bar graphs on blue
                      repeat their lines
                      glass tubes of boom
                      in concrete wicker
                      each trade Polaris
                      government Agena
                      fine print insurrected
                      tall drinks on a tray

All around them is the old order: brewery brick terrace hospital
horrible workplace; the scale of the tramway era,
the peajacket era, the age of the cliff-repeating woolstores.
South and west lie the treeless suburbs, a mulch of faded flags,
north and partly east, the built-in paradise forest.

3. *The flight from Manhattan*

It is possible the heights of this view are a museum
though the highrise continues desultorily along some ridges,
                canned Housing, Strata Title,
                see-through Office Space,
                upright bedsteads of Harbour View,
                residential soviets,
the cranes have all but vanished from the central upsurge.

                Hot-air money-driers,
                towering double entry,
                Freud's cobwebbed poem
                with revolving restaurant,

they took eighty years to fly here from Manhattan
these variant towers. By then, they were arriving everywhere.
                In the land of veneers,
                of cladding, of Cape Codding
                (I shall have Cape Codded)
                they put on heavy side.

The iron ball was loose in the old five-storey city
clearing bombsites for them. They rose like nouveaux accents
and stilled, for a time, the city's conversation.

                Their arrival paralleled
                the rise of the Consumers
                gazing through themselves
                at iconoclasms, wines,
                Danish Modern ethics.

Little we could love expanded to fill the spaces
of high glazed prosperity. An extensive city
that had long contained the dimensions of heaven and hell
couldn't manage total awe at the buildings of the Joneses.

                Their reign coincided
                with an updraft of ideology,
                that mood in which the starving
                spirit is fed upon the heart.

Employment and neckties and ruling themes ascended
into the towers. But they never filled them.
Squinting at them through the salt
and much-washed glass of her history, the city kept her flavour
fire-ladder high, rarely above three storeys.

In ambiguous battle at length, she began to hedge
the grilles of aspiration. To limit them to standing
on economic grounds. With their twists of sculpture.

On similar grounds we are stopped here, still surveying
the ridgy plain of houses. Enormous. England's buried Gulag.
The stacked entrepôt, great city of the Australians.

4. *The C19-20*

The Nineteenth Century. The Twentieth Century.
There were never any others. No centuries before these.
Dante was not hailed in his time as an Authentic
Fourteenth Century Voice. Nor did Cromwell thunder After all,
in the bowels of Christ, this *is* the Seventeenth Century.

The two are one aircraft in the end, the C19-20,
capacious with cargo. Some of it can save your life,
some can prevent it.
The cantilevered behemoth
is fitted up with hospitals and electric Gatling guns
to deal with recalcitrant and archaic spirits.

It rose out of the Nineteenth, steam pouring from venturi
and every man turning hay with a wooden fork
in the Age of Piety (AD or BC) wants one
in his nation's airline. And his children dream of living
in a palace of packing crates beside the cargo terminal:
No one will see! Everything will be surprises!

Directly under the flightpath, and tuned to listening,
we hear the cockpit traffic, the black box channel
that can't be switched off: Darwinians and Lawrentians
are wrestling for the controls,
We must take her into Space!/ We must fly in potent circles!

5. *The recession of the Joneses*

The worldwide breath of Catching Up
may serve to keep the mighty, slowing
machine aloft beyond our lifetime:
nearly all of the poor are blowing.

The soaring double century
might end, and mutate, and persist:
as we've been talking, the shadows of
bridges, cranes, towers have shifted east.

When we create our own high style
skill and the shadow will not then part;
as rhetoric would conceal from art
effort has at best a winning margin.

The sun, that is always catching up
with night and day and month and year
blazes from its scrolled bare face *To be
solar, I must be nuclear —*

Six hundred glittering and genteel towns
gathered to be urban in plein air,
more complex in their levels than their heights
and vibrant with modernity's strange anger.

Quintets for Robert Morley

Is it possible that hyper-
ventilating up Parnassus
I have neglected to pay tribute
to the Stone Age aristocracy?
   I refer to the fat.

We were probably the earliest
civilised, and civilising, humans,
the first to win the leisure,
sweet boredom, life-enhancing sprawl
   that require style.

Tribesfolk spared us and cared for us
for good reasons. Our reasons.
As age's counterfeits, forerunners of the city
we survived, and multiplied. Out of self-defence
   we invented the Self.

It's likely we also invented some of love,
much of fertility (see the Willensdorf Venus),
parts of theology (divine feasting, Unmoved Movers),
likewise complexity, stateliness, the ox-cart
   and self-deprecation.

Not that the lists of pugnacity are bare
of stout fellows. Ask a Sumo.
Warriors taunt us still, and fear us:
in heroic war, we're apt to be the specialists
   and the generals.

But we do better in peacetime. For ourselves
we would spare the earth. We were the first moderns
after all, being like the Common Man
disqualified from tragedy. Accessible to shame, though,
   subtler than the tall,

we make reasonable rulers.
Never trust a lean meritocracy
nor the leader who has been lean;
only the lifelong big have the knack of wedding
   greatness with balance.

Never wholly trust the fat man
who lurks in the lean achiever
and in the defeated, yearning to get out.
He has not been through our initiations,
   he lacks the light feet.

Our having life abundantly
is equivocal, Robert, in hot climates
where the hungry watch us. I lack the light step then too.
How many of us, I wonder, walk those streets
   in terrible disguise?

So much climbing, on a spherical world;
had Newton not been a mere beginner at gravity
he might have asked how the apple got up there
in the first place. And so might have discerned
   an ampler physics.

The New Moreton Bay

(on the conversion to Catholicism of the poet Kevin Hart)

A grog-primed overseer, who later died,
snapped at twenty convicts gasping in a line
That pole ain't heavy! Two men stand aside!
and then two more, *and you, pop-eyes! And you!*
— until the dozen left, with a terrible cry,
broke and were broken
beneath the tons of log they had stemmed aloft desperately.

Because there is no peace in this world's peace
the timber is to carry. Many hands heave customarily,
some step aside, detained by the Happiness Police
or despair's boutiques; it is a continual sway —
but when grace and intent
recruit a fresh shoulder, then we're in the other testament
and the innocent wood lifts line-long, with its leaves and libraries.

Anthropomorphics

Outside the serious media, the violence of animals
is often like a sad cartoon. Tom catches Jerry
and one of them grows less cute, glibbed with saliva,
shivering, darting. But Tom keeps his appealing intent look.
Similarly the snake, having struck and left you with it,
flourishes off quickly, his expression if anything self-righteous.
Hunting, we know, is mostly a form of shopping
where the problem's to make the packages hold still;
Death's best for that, though cheetahs have been seen feeding
on the bulk of a gazelle while the raised head end still bleated:
it was like the companionable sacking of a small Norse ship.
Even with sex, the symbolic beasts can be unreliable:
the great bull, mounting, cramps his lungs on her knobbed spine
and looks winded and precarious. He is more sexual walking.
I praise, nonetheless, our humane and Scythian arts.

The Romantic Theme of Ruins

The workmen clinked their steel, trudging; one murmured couplets
about a great house and chiefs beaten into the clay;
the new man rode ahead, engrossed with his new landscape
and the swell of his saddle. For ruins are the sleep of dynasty.

He met the neighbour heiress who, bored with church and luncheon,
had found in that gap of frost-spilled masonry
refuge from adulthood, then a precinct for the Numen —

Their children saw Earth itself as the great ruin:
was she not the contracted wreck of Chaos? and of the Spiral
that is primal Order? They walked her final patina.
Travelling, delving, they found themselves everywhere in it.

As dramatic buildings encroached, including their own,
their houses assumed a shade of ruin, a domesticated patina.
Breeding shone in slight defeat. They opposed the soaring line
with a settled, undulant, edge-abraded line Earth taught them.

Ruins lacked all charm, though, closest to home, in the flesh:
gallows-fruit, senility of parents, the bottle-wrapped veteran
wobbling in the lane, his face like matted genitals —

You are too inclusive, they cried. You overwork a metaphor!
Ruins are not Christian. They are sober poignant spirits;
they are the afterlife of genteel religion.

Descendants, by this time, were riding beside battalions
of steel-clinking workmen, going to make ruins
and establish, they said, a line of common nobility.
The spiral now contracted faster. Generations

cried out to each other from their collapsing levels.
We were above this! and heard the answering laughter,
These ruins are heroic! and heard the avenging answer.

Ruins and tribes and wilderness merged thereafter
and all the trusted creatures. Earth became the Great Museum
whose other, more secret name is Noble Conquest.

It swarmed with new people, steel in the hands of some
and in the blood of others. Hey, off with your gentilities!
we're your new ruins, they cried, we're the water sign!
and this is the true dance, the Beat, helix of Helikon!

Lies and the truth, said Nine there, the truth and lies,

we purvey both. You want truth? Just the one?
Truth may be lacking in flair for your aristocracies,
and it tends to be successive, with your orthodocracies;
for instance, now Ruins: for our next intimation . . .

Bent Water in the Tasmanian Highlands

Flashy wrists out of buttoned grass cuffs, feral whisky burning gravels,
jazzy knuckles ajitter on soakages, peaty cupfulls, soft pots overflowing,
setting out along the great curve, migrating mouse-quivering water,
mountain-driven winter water, in the high tweed, stripping off its mountains
to run faster in its skin, it swallows the above, it feeds where it is fed on,
it forms at many points and creases outwards, pleated water
shaking out its bedding soil, increasing its scale, beginning the headlong
— Bent Water, you could call this level
between droplet and planetary, not as steered by twisting beds laterally
but as upped and swayed on its swelling and outstanding own curvatures,
its floating top that sweeps impacts sidelong, its event-horizon,
a harelip round a pebble, mouthless cheeks globed over a boulder, a
finger's far-stretched holograph, skinned flow athwart a snag
— these flexures are all reflections, motion-glyphs, pitches of impediment,
say a log commemorated in a log-long hump of wave,
a buried rock continually noted, a squeeze-play
through a cracked basalt bar, maintaining a foam-roofed two-sided
overhang of breakneck riesling; uplifted hoseless hosings, fully circular water,
flattened water off rock sills, sandwiched between an upper
and a lower whizzing surface, trapped in there with airy scatter
and mingled high-speed mirrorings; water groined, produced and spiralled
— Crowded scrollwork from events, at steepening white velocities
as if the whole outline of the high country were being pulled out
along these joining channels, and proving infinite, anchored deeply as it is
in the groundwater scale, in the silence around racy breccia,
yet it is spooling out; the great curve, drawing and driving,
of which these are the animal-sized swells and embodiments
won't always describe this upland; and after the jut falls, the inverse
towering on gorges, these peaks will be hidden beneath
rivers and tree-bark, in electricity, in cattle, on the ocean
— Meditation is a standing wave, though, on the black-green inclines
of pouring and cascading, slate-dark rush and timberworker's tea
bullying the pebble-fans; if we were sketched first at this speed,
sheaths, buttocks, wings, it is mother and history and swank here
till our wave is drained of water. And as such it includes the writhing
down in a trench, knees, bellies, the struggling, the slack bleeding
remote enough perhaps, within its close clean film
to make the observer a god; do we come here to be gods?
or to watch an alien pouring down the slants of our anomaly
and be hypnotised to rest by it? So much detail's unlikely, for hypnosis;
it looks like brotherhood sought at a dreamer's remove
and, in either view, laws of falling and persistence:
the continuous ocean round a planetary stone, braiding uptilts
after swoops, echo-forms, arches built from above and standing
on flourish, clear storeys, translucent honey-glazed clerestories —

Equanimity

Nests of golden porridge shattered in the silky-oak trees,
cobs and crusts of it, their glory box;
the jacarandas' open violet immensities
mirrored flat on the lawns,
weighted by sprinklers; birds, singly and in flocks
hopping over the suburb, eating, as birds do, in detail
and paying their peppercorns;
talk of "the good life" tangles love with will
however; if we mention it, there is more to say:
the droughty light, for example, at telephone-wire
height above the carports, not the middle-ground
distilling news-photograph light of a smoggy Wednesday,
but that light of the north-west wind, hung on the sky
like the haze above cattleyards;
hungry mountain birds, too, drifting in for food, with the sound
of moist gullies about them, and the sound of the pinch-bar;
we must hear the profoundly unwished
garble of a neighbours' quarrel, and see repeatedly
the face we saw near the sportswear shop today
in which mouth-watering and tears couldn't be distinguished.

Fire-prone place-names apart
there is only love; there are no Arcadias.
Whatever its variants of meat-cuisine, worship, divorce,
human order has at heart
an equanimity. Quite different from inertia, it's a place
where the churchman's not defensive, the indignant aren't on the qui vive,
the loser has lost interest, the accountant is truant to remorse,
where the farmer has done enough struggling-to-survive
for one day, and the artist rests from theory —
where all are, in short, off the high comparative horse
of their identity.
Almost beneath notice, as attainable as gravity, it is
a continuous recovering moment. Pity the high madness
that misses it continually, ranging without rest between
assertion and unconsciousness,
the sort that makes hell seem a height of evolution.
Through the peace beneath effort
(even within effort: quiet air between the bars of our attention)
comes unpurchased lifelong plenishment;
Christ spoke to people most often on this level
especially when they chattered about kingship and the Romans;
all holiness speaks from it.

From the otherworld of action and media, this
interleaved continuing plane is hard to focus:
we are looking into the light —
it makes some smile, some grimace.
More natural to look at the birds about the street, their life
that is greedy, pinched, courageous and prudential
as any on these bricked tree-mingled miles of settlement,
to watch the unceasing on-off
grace that attends their nearly every movement,
the crimson parrot has it, alighting, tips, and recovers it,
the same grace moveless in the shapes of trees
and complex in our selves and fellow walkers; we see it's indivisible
and scarcely willed. That it lights us from the incommensurable
we sometimes glimpse, from being trapped in the point
(bird minds and ours are so pointedly visual):
a field all foreground, and equally all background,
like a painting of equality. Of infinite detailed extent
like God's attention. Where nothing is diminished by perspective.

The Forest Hit by Modern Use

The forest, hit by modern use,
stands graced with damage.
                          Angled plaques
tilt everywhere, with graphic needle crowns
and trinket saps fixed round their year;
vines spiderweb, flowering, over smashed
intricacies; long rides appear.

Dense growths that were always underbrush
expand in the light, beside bulldozers'
imprinted machine-gun belts of spoor.

Now the sun's in, through breaks and jags,
culled slopes are jammed with replacement; green
and whipstick saplings, every one out
to shade the rest to death.
                         Scabbed chain
feeds leaf-mould its taut rain-cold solution;
bared creeks wash gold; kingfishers hover.

There is still great height: all through the hills
spared hierarchs toughen to the wind
around the punk hearts that got them spared
and scatter seed down the logging roads.

Grease-fungi, scrolls, clenched pipes of bark:
the forest will now be kept like this
for a long time. There are rooms in it
and, paradox for mystery, birds
too tiny, now that we see them, for
their amplitude and carrying flash of song.

On a stump, a sea eagle eats by lengths
their enemy, a coil-whipping dry land fish
and voids white size to make room for it.

Shower

From the metal poppy
this good blast of trance
arriving as shock, private cloudburst blazing down,
worst in a boarding-house greased tub, or a barrack with competitions,
best in a stall, this enveloping passion of Australians:
tropics that sweat for you, torrent that braces with its heat,
inflames you with its chill, action sauna, inverse bidet,
sleek vertical coruscating ghost of your inner river,
reminding all your fluids, streaming off your points, awakening
the tacky soap to blossom and ripe autumn, releasing the squeezed gardens,
smoky valet smoothing your impalpable overnight pyjamas off,
pillar you can step through, force-field absolving love's efforts,
nicest yard of the jogging track, speeding aeroplane minutely
steered with two controls, or trimmed with a knurled wheel.
Some people like to still this energy and lie in it,
stirring circles with their pleasure in it — but my delight's that toga
worn on either or both shoulders, fluted drapery, silk whispering to the tiles
with its spiralling frothy hem continuous round the gurgle-hole;
this ecstatic partner, dreamy to dance in slow embrace with
after factory-floor rock, or even to meet as Lot's abstracted
merciful wife on a rusty ship in dog latitudes,
sweetest dressing of the day in the dusty bush, this persistent
time-capsule of unwinding, this nimble straight well-wisher.
Only in England is its name an unkind word;
only in Europe is it enjoyed by telephone.

The Quality of Sprawl

Sprawl is the quality
of the man who cut down his Rolls-Royce
into a farm utility truck, and sprawl
is what the company lacked when it made repeated efforts
to buy the vehicle back and repair its image.

Sprawl is doing your farming by aeroplane, roughly,
or driving a hitchhiker that extra hundred miles home.
It is the rococo of being your own still centre.
It is never lighting cigars with ten-dollar notes:
that's idiot ostentation and murder of starving people.
Nor can it be bought with the ash of million-dollar deeds.

Sprawl lengthens the legs; it trains greyhounds on liver and beer.
Sprawl almost never says Why not? with palms comically raised
nor can it be dressed for, not even in running shoes worn
with mink and a nose ring. That is Society. That's Style.
Sprawl is more like the thirteenth banana in a dozen
or anyway the fourteenth.

Sprawl is Hank Stamper in Never Give an Inch
bisecting an obstructive official's desk with a chain saw.
Not harming the official. Sprawl is never brutal
though it's often intransigent. Sprawl is never Simon de Montfort
at a town-storming: Kill them all! God will know his own.
Knowing the man's name this was said to might be sprawl.

Sprawl occurs in art. The fifteenth to twenty-first
lines in a sonnet, for example. And in certain paintings;
I have sprawl enough to have forgotten which paintings.
Turner's glorious Burning of the Houses of Parliament
comes to mind, a doubling bannered triumph of sprawl —
except, he didn't fire them.

Sprawl gets up the nose of many kinds of people
(every kind that comes in kinds) whose futures don't include it.
Some decry it as criminal presumption, silken-robed Pope Alexander
dividing the new world between Spain and Portugal.
If he smiled *in petto* afterwards, perhaps the thing did have sprawl.

Sprawl is really classless, though. It's John Christopher Frederick Murray
asleep in his neighbours' best bed in spurs and oilskins
but not having thrown up:
sprawl is never Calum who, in the loud hallway of our house,
reinvented the Festoon. Rather
it's Beatrice Miles going twelve hundred ditto in a taxi,

No Lewd Advances, No Hitting Animals, No Speeding,
on the proceeds of her two-bob-a-sonnet Shakespeare readings.
An image of my country. And would that it were more so.

No, sprawl is full-gloss murals on a council-house wall.
Sprawl leans on things. It is loose-limbed in its mind.
Reprimanded and dismissed
it listens with a grin and one boot up on the rail
of possibility. It may have to leave the Earth.
Being roughly Christian, it scratches the other cheek
and thinks it unlikely. Though people have been shot for sprawl.

Three Poems in Memory of My Mother, Miriam Murray née Arnall

Born 23.5.1915, died 19.4.1951

Weights

Not owning a cart, my father
in the drought years was a bowing
green hut of cattle feed, moving,
or gasping under cream cans. No weight
would he let my mother carry.

Instead, she wielded handles
in the kitchen and dairy, singing often,
gave saucepan-boiled injections
with her ward-sister skill, nursed neighbours,
scorned gossips, ran committees.

She gave me her factual tone,
her facial bones, her will,
not her beautiful voice
but her straightness and her clarity.

I did not know back then
nor for many years what it was,
after me, she could not carry.

Midsummer Ice

Remember how I used
to carry ice in from the road
for the ice chest, half running,
the white rectangle clamped in bare hands
the only utter cold
in all those summer paddocks?

How, swaying, I'd hurry it inside
en bloc and watering, with the butter
and the wrapped bread precarious on top of it?
"Poor Leslie," you would say,
"your hands are cold as charity —"
You made me take the barrow
but uphill it was heavy.

We'd no tongs, and a bag
would have soaked and bumped, off balance.
I loved to eat the ice,
chip it out with the butcher knife's grey steel.
It stopped good things rotting
and it had a strange comb at its heart,
a splintered horizon rife with zero pearls.

But you don't remember.
A doorstep of numbed creek water the colour of tears
but you don't remember.
I will have to die before you remember.

The Steel

I am older than my mother.
Cold steel hurried me from her womb.
I haven't got a star.

What hour I followed
the waters into this world
no one living can now say.
My zodiac got washed away.

The steel of my induction
killed my brothers and sisters;
once or twice I was readied for them

and then they were not mentioned
again, at the hospital
to me or to the visitors.
The reticence left me only.

I think, apart from this,
my parents' life was happy,
provisional, as lives are.

Farming spared them from the war,
that, and an ill-knit blue shin
my father had been harried back

to tree-felling with, by his father
who supervised from horseback.
The times were late pioneer.

So was our bare plank house
with its rain stains down each crack
like tall tan flames,
magic swords, far matched perspectives:

it reaped Dad's shamed invectives —
Paying him rent for this shack!
The landlord was his father.

But we also had fireside ease,
health, plentiful dinners, the radio;
we'd a car to drive to tennis.

Country people have cars
for more than shopping and show,
our Dodge reached voting age, though,
in my first high school year.

I was in the town at school
the afternoon my mother
collapsed, and was carried from the dairy.
The car was out of order.

The ambulance was available
but it took a doctor's say-so
to come. This was refused.
My father pleaded. Was refused.

The local teacher's car was got finally.
The time all this took didn't pass,
it spread through sheets, unstoppable.

Thirty-seven miles to town
and the terrible delay.
Little blood brother, blood sister,
I don't blame you.
How can you blame a baby?
or the longing for a baby?

Little of that week
comes back. The vertigo,
the apparent recovery —
She will get better now.
The relapse on the Thursday.

In school and called away
I was haunted, all that week,
by the spectre of dark women,
Murrays dressed in midday black

who lived on the river islands
and are seen only at funerals;
their terrible weak authority.

Everybody in the town
was asking me about my mother;
I could only answer childishly
to them. And to my mother,

and on Friday afternoon
our family world
went inside itself forever.

Sister Arnall, city girl
with your curt good sense
were you being the nurse
when you let them hurry me?
being responsible

when I was brought on to make way
for a difficult birth in that cottage hospital
and the Cheers child stole my birthday?

Or was it our strange diffidence,
unworldly at a pinch, unresentful,
being a case among cases,

a relative, wartime sense,
modern, alien to fuss,
that is not in the Murrays?

I don't blame the Cheers boy's mother:
she didn't put her case.
It was the steel proposed
reasonably, professionally,
that became your sentence

but I don't decry unselfishness:
I'm proud of it. Of you.
Any virtue can be fatal.

In the event, his coming gave no trouble
but it might have, I agree;
nothing you agreed to harmed me.
I didn't mean to harm you
I was a baby.

For a long time, my father
himself became a baby
being perhaps wiser than me,
less modern, less military;

he was not ashamed of grief,
of its looking like a birth
out through the face

bloated, whiskery, bringing no relief.
It was mainly through fear
that I was at times his father.
I have long been sorry.

Caked pans, rancid blankets,
despair and childish cool
were our road to Bohemia
that bitter wartime country.

What were you thinking of,
Doctor MB, BS?
Were you very tired?
Did you have more pressing cases?

Know panic when you heard it:
Oh you can bring her in!
Did you often do
diagnosis by telephone?

Perhaps we wrong you,
make a scapegoat of you;
perhaps there was no stain
of class in your decision,

no view that two framed degrees
outweighed a dairy.
It's nothing, dear:
just some excited hillbilly —

As your practice disappeared
and you were cold-shouldered in town
till you broke and fled,
did you think of the word Clan?

It is an antique
concept. But not wholly romantic.
We came to the river early;
it gives us some protection.

You'll agree the need is real.
I can forgive you now
and not to seem magnanimous.
It's enough that you blundered
on our family steel.

Thirty-five years on earth:
that's short. That's short, Mother,
as the lives cut off by war

and the lives of spilt children are short.
Justice wholly in this world
would bring them no rebirth
nor restore your latter birthdays.
How could that be justice?

My father never quite
remarried. He went back
by stages of kindness to me
to the age of lonely men,
of only men, and men's company

that is called the Pioneer age.
Snig chain and mountain track;
he went back to felling trees

and seeking justice from his
dead father. His only weakness.
One's life is not a case

except of course it is.
Being just, seeking justice:
they were both of them right,
my mother and my father.

There is justice, there is death,
humanist: you can't have both.
Activist, you can't serve both.
You do not move in measured space.

The poor man's anger is a prayer
for equities Time cannot hold
and steel grows from our mother's grace.
Justice is the people's otherworld.

Machine Portraits with Pendant Spaceman

For Valerie

The bulldozer stands short as a boot on its heel-high ripple soles;
it has toecapped stumps aside all day, scuffed earth and trampled rocks
making a hobnailed dyke downstream of raw clay shoals.
Its work will hold water. The man who bounced high on the box
seat, exercising levers, would swear a full frontal orthodox
oath to that. First he shaved off the grizzled scrub
with that front-end safety razor supplied by the school of hard knocks
then he knuckled down and ground his irons properly; they copped many a
                                                                                                      harsh rub.
At knock-off time, spilling thunder, he surfaced like a sub.

    — o —

Speaking of razors, the workshop amazes with its strop,
its elapsing leather drive-belt angled to the slapstick flow
of fast work in the Chaplin age; tightened, it runs like syrup,
streams like a mill-sluice, fiddles like a glazed virtuoso.
With the straitlaced summary cut of Sam Brownes long ago
it is the last of the drawn lash and bullocking muscle
left in engineering. It's where the panther leaping, his swift shadow
and all such free images turned plastic. Here they dwindle, dense with oil,
like a skein between tough factory hands, pulley and diesel.

    — o —

Shaking in slow low flight, with its span of many jets,
the combine seeder at nightfall swimming over flat land
is a style of machinery we'd imagined for the fictional planets:
in the high glassed cabin, above vapour-pencilling floodlights, a hand,
gloved against the cold, hunts along the medium-wave band
for company of Earth voices; it crosses speech garble music —
the Brandenburg Conch the Who the Illyrian High Command —
as seed wheat in the hoppers shakes down, being laced into the thick
night-dampening plains soil, and the stars waver out and stick.

    — o —

Flags and a taut fence discipline the mountain pasture
where giant upturned mushrooms gape mildly at the sky
catching otherworld pollen. Poppy-smooth or waffle-ironed, each armature
distils wild and white sound. These, Earth's first antennae
tranquilly angled outwards, to a black, not a gold infinity,
swallow the millionfold numbers that print out as a risen
glorious Apollo. They speak control to satellites in high
bursts of algorithm. And some of them are tuned to win
answers to fair questions, viz. What is the Universe in?

— O —

How many metal-bra and trumpet-flaring film extravaganzas
underlie the progress of the space shuttle's Ground Transporter Vehicle
across macadam-surfaced Florida? Atop oncreeping house-high panzers,
towering drydock and ocean-liner decks, there perches a gridiron football
field in gradual motion; it is the god-platform; it sustains the bridal
skyscraper of liquid Cool, and the rockets borrowed from the Superman
and the bricked aeroplane of Bustout-and-return, all vertical,
conjoined and myth-huge, approaching the starred gantry where human
lightning will crack, extend, and vanish upwards from this caravan.

— O —

        Gold-masked, the foetal warrior
        unslipping on a flawless floor,
        I backpack air; my life machine
        breathes me head-Earthwards, speaks the Choctaw
        of tech-talk that earths our discipline —

        but the home world now seems outside-in;
        I marvel that here background's so fore
        and sheathe my arms in the unseen

        a dream in images unrecalled
        from any past takes me   I soar
        at the heart of fall on a drifting line

        this is the nearest I have been
        to oneness with the everted world
        the unsinking leap   the stone unfurled

— O —

In a derelict village picture show I will find a projector,
dust-matted, but with film in its drum magazines, and the lens
mysteriously clean. The film will be called *Insensate Violence*,
no plot, no characters, just shoot burn scream beg claw
bayonet trample brains — I will hit the reverse switch then, in conscience,
and the thing will run backwards, unlike its coeval the machine-gun;
blood will unspill, fighters lift and surge apart; horror will be undone
and I will come out to a large town, bright parrots round the saleyard pens
and my people's faces healed of a bitter sophistication.

— O —

The more I act, the stiller I become;
the less I'm lit, the more spellbound my crowd;
I accept all colours, and with a warming hum
I turn them white and hide them in a cloud.
To give long life is a power I'm allowed
by my servant, Death. I am what you can't sell
at the world's end — and if you're still beetle-browed
try some of my treasures: an adult bird in its shell
or a pink porker in his own gut, Fritz the Abstract Animal.

— O —

No riddles about a crane. This one drops a black clanger on cars
and the palm of its four-thumbed steel hand is a raptor of wrecked tubing;
the ones up the highway hoist porridgy concrete, long spars
and the local skyline; whether raising aloft on a string
bizarre workaday angels, or letting down a rotating
man on a sphere, these machines are inclined to maintain
a peace like world war, in which we turn over everything
to provide unceasing victories. Now the fluent lines stop, and strain
engrosses this tower on the frontier of junk, this crane.

— O —

Before a landscape sprouts those giant stepladders that pump oil
or before far out iron mosquitoes attach to the sea
there is this sortilege with phones that plug into mapped soil,
the odd gelignite bump to shake trucks, paper scribbling out serially
as men dial Barrier Reefs long enfolded beneath the geology
or listen for black Freudian beaches; they seek a miles-wide pustular
rock dome of pure Crude, a St Paul's-in-profundis. There are many
wrong numbers on the geophone, but it's brought us some distance, and by car.
Every machine has been love and a true answer.

— O —

Not a high studded ship boiling cauliflower under her keel
nor a ghost in bootlaced canvas — just a length of country road
afloat between two shores, winding wet wire rope reel-to-reel,
dismissing romance sternwards. Six cars and a hay truck are her load
plus a thoughtful human cast which could, in some dramatic episode,
become a world. All machines in the end join God's creation
growing bygone, given, changeless — but a river ferry has its timeless mode
from the grinding reedy outset; it enforces contemplation.
We arrive. We traverse depth in thudding silence. We go on.

The International Poetry Festivals Thing

Those conventions of the trade
in affluent stone cities:
we travel to them up the long shaft
polished by Europe's victims;

since few books can ascend that,
we walk out past the airport submachine-guns
carrying the mirrors we hold up
to the life of our people.

Those scenes at the first
usually luxurious breakfast:
Ciao Allen! Zhenia moi!
polished brevity of attention,
hooded senior repartee,
witty switching of small table flags

but always the unspoken
question, too: how many
divisions, with that fellow?

You notice, on lone walks,
how the city was rebuilt.
Yet you do the unspeakable

among competitive nonchalances
and the polite who've seen Hell:
you are unguarded.
No one is that distinguished!

At last the readings,
super-cool or impassioned recitals
very largely of subtitles
even in fair translation.

Hour on stylish hour of it:
Who is to read now — the Pole?
No, the opposite Pole —
Nothing worthwhile is lost:
the poetry is in print somewhere.

And afterwards, always,
an Englishman quoting cliché
with a heavy archness,
often doing it out of friendliness.

Some things do get through,
your relief at quiet praise
tells you how unguarded
you really were not, previously.

To your terror, you find
you have earned the admiration
of that bright girl who
for always coming down on one side
you had nicknamed Winter Sunlight:

now you may have to say it —
*il me serait trop
distingué, ton prolétariat* —

Meanwhile, the spirit follows
its curious own nose
collecting, for its lasting life,
south sun. A Gothic square.
Café lamps. Two conversations.
Icecreamed tongues in the horse chestnut trees.

Declining, conjugating,
the week ends in embraces
of love, of career,
Will you be now in Cambridge?
in real regard and book exchanges.

And we carry home our sleek
mirrors cram-full of chic
to show our people.

Little Boy Impelling a Scooter

Little boy on a wet pavement
near nightfall, balancing his scooter,
his free foot spurning it along,
his every speeding touchdown
striking a match of spent light,
the long concrete patched with squeezed-dry impacts
coming and going, his tyres' rubber edge
splitting the fine water. He jinks the handlebars
and trots around them, turning them
back, and stamps fresh small impulsions
maddeningly on and near, off and behind
his earlier impulses.
                        Void blurring pavement stars,
void blurring wheel-noise, uneven with hemmed outsets
as the dark deepens over town. To bear his rapture,
to smile, to share in it, require attitudes
all remote from murder,
watching his bowed intent face and slackly trailing
sudden pump leg passing and hemm! repassing
under powerlines and windy leaves
and the bared night sky's interminable splendours.

Self-Portrait from a Photograph

If this picture has survived
its subject's absorption in the absolute
which is either God or death

it will first have been obsolete
for many years, till its style
was wholly defused, its life

glazed over by pathos, by summary
and it could grow timeless,
a midcentury face, taken late in that century.

A high hill of photographed sun-shadow
coming up from reverie, the big head
has its eyes on a mid-line, the mouth
slightly open, to breathe or interrupt.

The face's gentle skew to the left
is abetted, or caused, beneath the nose
by a Heidelberg scar, got in an accident.
The hair no longer meets across the head

and the back and sides are clipped ancestrally
Puritan-short. The chins are firm and deep
respectively. In point of freckling
the bare and shaven skin is just over

halfway between childhood ginger
and the nutmeg and plastic death-mottle
of great age. The large ears suggest more
of the soul than the other features:

dull to speech, alert to language,
tuned to background rustle, easily agonised,
all too fond of monotony, they help
keep the eyes, at their sharpest, remote,

half-turned to another world
that is poorer than this one, but contains it.
The short bulb nose is propped firmly
by flesh ridges. In decline, slow or steep,

this face might have wrinkled copiously
by the shoalwater webbing near the eyes.
With temples this military-naked
you see muscles chewing in the head.

That look of dawning interest, or objection
in which we glimpse dread of dentists
could be shifting to enjoy a corny joke
out of friendship, or in reflex defiance

of claimant Good Taste and display;
such moods were one edge of his loyalty.
Another is the biceps tourniquet
of rolled sleeves, just out of frame,

a fashion of darkening carriers,
farmers, labourers and their sons
for more than a century.

Wardrobe, this precise relation
between a pinstriped business shirt
and its absent tie can never be recaptured,

and slighter factors, in this drapery and skin:
like impulses deflected by the saints
they end here, short of history.

The Hypogeum

Below the moveable gardens of this shopping centre
down concrete ways
                to a level of rainwater,
a black lake glimmering among piers, electric lighted,
windless, of no depth.
                Rare shafts of daylight
waver at their base. As the water is shaken, the few
cars parked down here seem to rock. In everything
there strains that silent crash, that reverberation
which persists in concrete.
                The cardboard carton
Lorenzo's Natural Flavour Italian Meat Balls has foundered
into a wet ruin. Dutch Cleanser is propped at a high
featureless wall. Self-Raising Flour is still floating
and supermarket trolleys hang their inverse harps,
silver leaking from them.
                What will help the informally religious
to endure peace? Surface water dripping into
this underworld makes now a musical blip,
now rings from nowhere.
                Young people descending the ramp
pause at the water's brink, banging their voices.

An Immortal

Beckoner of hotheads, brag-tester, lord of the demi-suicides,
in only one way since far before Homer have you altered:
when now, on wry wheels still revolving, the tall dust showers back
and tongue-numbing Death stills a screaming among the jagged images,
you disdain to strip your victims' costly armour, bright with fire and duco
or even to step forth, visible briefly in your delusive harness,
glass cubes whirling at your tread, the kinked spear of frenzy in your hand.

Do you appear, though, bodily to your vanquished challengers
with the bare face of the boy who was large and quickest at it,
the hard face of the boss and the bookie, strangely run together,
the face of the expert craftsman, smiling privately, shaking his head?
Are you sometimes the Beloved, approaching and receding through the glaze?
Or is this all merely cinema? Are your final interviews wholly personal
and the bolt eyes disjunct teeth blood-vomit all a kind mask lent by physics?

We will never find out, living. The volunteers, wavering and firm,
and the many conscripted to storm the house of meaning
have stayed inside, with the music. Or else they are ourselves,
sheepish, reminiscent, unsure how we made it past the Warrior
into our lives — which the glory of his wheeled blade has infected
so that, on vacant evenings, we may burn with the mystery of his face,
his speed, his streetlights pointing every way, his unbelief in joking.

Second Essay on Interest: The Emu

Weathered blond as a grass tree, a huge Beatles haircut
raises an alert periscope and stares out
over scrub. Her large olivine eggs click
oilily together; her lips of noble plastic
clamped in their expression, her head-fluff a stripe
worn mohawk style, she bubbles her pale-blue windpipe:
the emu, *Dromaius novaehollandiae*,
whose stand-in on most continents is an antelope,
looks us in both eyes with her one eye
and her other eye, dignified courageous hump,
feather-swaying condensed camel, Swift Courser of New Holland.

Knees backward in toothed three-way boots, you stand,
Dinewan, proud emu, common as the dust
in your sleeveless cloak, returning our interest.
Your shield of fashion's wobbly: you're Quaint, you're Native,
even somewhat Bygone. You may be let live
but beware: the blank zones of Serious disdain
are often carte blanche to the darkly human.
Europe's boats on their first strange shore looked humble
but, Mass over, men started renaming the creatures.
Worship turned to interest and had new features.
Now only life survives, if it's made remarkable.

Heraldic bird, our protection is a fable
made of space and neglect. We're remarkable and not;
we're the ordinary discovered on a strange planet.
Are you Early or Late, in the history of birds
which doesn't exist, and is deeply ancient?
My kinships, too, are immemorial and recent,
like my country, which abstracts yours in words.
This distillate of mountains is finely branched, this plain
expanse of dour delicate lives, where the rain,
shrouded slab on the west horizon, is a corrugated revenant
settling its long clay-tipped plumage in a hatching descent.

Rubberneck, stepped sister, I see your eye on our jeep's load.
I think your story is, when you were offered
the hand of evolution, you gulped it. Forefinger and thumb
project from your face, but the weighing palm is inside you
collecting the bottletops, nails, wet cement that you famously swallow,
your passing muffled show, your serially private museum.
Some truths are now called *trivial*, though. Only God approves them.
Some humans who disdain them make a kind of weather
which, when it grows overt and widespread, we call *war*.
There we make death trivial and awesome, by rapid turns about,
we conscript it to bless us, force-feed it to squeeze the drama out;

indeed we imprison and torture death — this part is called *peace* —
we offer it murder like mendicants, begging for significance.
You rustle dreams of pardon, not fleeing in your hovercraft style,
not gliding fast with zinc-flaked legs dangling, feet making high-tensile
seesawing impacts. Wasteland parent, barely edible dignitary,
the disinterested spotlight of the lords of interest
and gowned nobles of ennui is a torch of vivid arrest
and blinding after-darkness. But you hint it's a brigand sovereignty
after the steady extents of God's common immortality
whose image is daylight detail, aggregate, in process yet plumb
to the everywhere focus of one devoid of boredom.

A Retrospect of Humidity

All the air conditioners now slacken
their hummed carrier wave. Once again
we've served our three months with remissions
in the steam and dry iron of this seaboard.
In jellied glare, through the nettle-rash season
we've watched the sky's fermenting laundry
portend downpours. Some came, and steamed away,
and we were clutched back into the rancid
saline midnights of orifice weather,
to damp grittiness and wiping off the air.

Metaphors slump irritably together in
the muggy weeks. Shark and jellyfish shallows
become suburbs where you breathe a fat towel;
babies burst like tomatoes with discomfort
in the cotton-wrapped pointing street markets;
the Lycra-bulging surf drips from non-swimmers
miles from shore, and somehow includes soil.
Skins, touching, soak each other. Skin touching
any surface wets that and itself
in a kind of mutual digestion.
Throbbing heads grow lianas of nonsense.

It's our annual visit to the latitudes
of rice, kerosene and resignation,
an averted, temporary visit
unrelated, for most, to the attitudes
of festive northbound jets gaining height —
closer, for some few, to the memory
of ulcers scraped with a tin spoon
or sweated faces bowing before dry
where the flesh is worn inside out,
all the hunger-organs clutched in rank nylon,
by those for whom exhaustion is spirit:

an intrusive, heart-narrowing season
at this far southern foot of the monsoon.
As the kleenex flower, the hibiscus
drops its browning wads, we forget
annually, as one forgets a sickness.
The stifling days will never come again,
not now that we've seen the first sweater
tugged down on the beauties of division
and inside the rain's millions, a risen
loaf of cat on a cool night veranda.

Flowering Eucalypt in Autumn

That slim creek out of the sky
the dried-blood western gum tree
is all stir in its high reaches:

its strung haze-blue foliage is dancing
points down in breezy mobs, swapping
pace and place in an all-over sway

retarded en masse by crimson blossom.
Bees still at work up there tack
around their exploded furry likeness

and the lawn underneath's a napped rug
of eyelash drift, of blooms flared
like a sneeze in a redhaired nostril,

minute urns, pinch-sized rockets
knocked down by winds, by night-creaking
fig-squirting bats, or the daily

parrot gang with green pocketknife wings.
Bristling food for tough delicate
raucous life, each flower comes

as a spray in its own turned vase,
a taut starburst, honeyed model
of the tree's fragrance crisping in your head.

When the Japanese plum tree
was shedding in spring, we speculated
there among the drizzling petals

what kind of exquisitely precious
artistic bloom might be gendered
in a pure ethereal compost

of petals potted as they fell.
From unpetalled gum-debris
we know what is grown continually,

a tower of fabulous swish tatters,
a map hoisted upright, a crusted
riverbed with up-country show towns.

The Chimes of Niegeschah

The timeless state of Niegeschah
is hard to place as near or far
since all things which didn't take place are there
and things which have lost the place they took:

Herr Hitler's buildings, King James' cigar,
the happiness of Armenia,
plump Madame Héloise Abelard
are there with the Pictish Grammar Book.

The girl who returned your dazzled look
and the mornings you might have passed with her
have built you a house in Niegeschah.
There shine the dukes of Australia

and all the great poems that never were
quite written, and every balked idea.
There too are the Third AIF and its war
in which I and boys of my age were killed

more pointlessly with each passing year.
There, too, half the works of sainthood are,
the enslavements, tortures, rapes, despair
which they deflected from this world

to join the failed hopes and similar
treasures of the region's avatar,
the utopian, the ubiquitous one,
our image reversed and singular,

the comet's plume that shuns its star.
With his eye for everything undone
he dotes on the spoils of Niegeschah
and stirs and whirls with his long finned car

the ash of enormities forestalled
and blows it, through various media,
into this obverse actual sphere
where all the real horrors have occurred

though not each time, nor everywhere
but which he'd make desperate, grey and blurred,
weighed down and raging towards that hour
which he has derided and longed for
when the singular shall meet the sole
Ultimate who is not from Niegeschah:

the One who is in this world and next
as poetry is in the text,
the mystery that confers reality
and details the proud constructs away.

The Smell of Coal Smoke

John Brown, glowing far and down,
wartime Newcastle was a brown town,
handrolled cough and cardigan, rain on paving bricks,
big smoke to a four-year-old from the green sticks.
Train city, mother's city, coming on dark,
Japanese shell holes awesome in a park,
electric light and upstairs, encountered first that day,
sailors and funny ladies in Jerry's Fish Café.

It is always evening on those earliest trips,
raining through the tram wires where blue glare rips
across the gaze of wonderment and leaves thrilling tips.
The steelworks' vast roofed débris unrolling falls
of smoky stunning orange, its eye-hurting slump walls
mellow to lounge interiors, cut pile and curry-brown
with the Pears-Soap-smelling fire and a sense of ships
mourning to each other below in the town.

This was my mother's childhood and her difference,
her city-brisk relations who valued Sense
talking strike and colliery, engineering, fowls and war,
Brown's grit and miners breathing it, years before
as I sat near the fire, raptly touching coal,
its blockage, slick yet dusty, prisms massed and dense
in the iron scuttle, its hammered bulky roll
into the glaring grate to fracture and shoal,

its chips you couldn't draw with on the cement
made it a stone, tar crockery, different —
and I had three grandparents, while others had four:
where was my mother's father, never called Poor?
In his tie and his Vauxhall that had a boat bow
driving up the Coalfields, but where was he now?
Coal smoke as much as gum trees now had a tight scent
to summon deep brown evenings of the Japanese war,

to conjure gaslit pub yards, their razory frisson
and sense my dead grandfather, the Grafton Cornishman
rising through the night schools by the pressure in his chest
as his lungs creaked like mahogany with the grains of John Brown.
His city, mother's city, at its starriest
as swearing men with doctors' bags streamed by toward the docks
past the smoke-frothing wooden train that would take us home soon
with our day-old Henholme chickens peeping in their box.

The Mouthless Image of God in the Hunter-Colo Mountains

Starting a dog, in the past-midnight suburbs, for a laugh,
barking for a lark, or to nark and miff, being tough
or dumbly meditative, starting gruff, sparking one dog off
almost companionably, you work him up, playing the rough riff
of punkish mischief, get funky as a poultry-farm diff
and vary with the Prussian note: *Achtung! Schar, Gewehr' auf!*
starting all the dogs off, for the tinny chain reaction and stiff
far-spreading music, the backyard territorial guff
echoing off brick streets, garbage cans, off every sandstone cliff
in miles-wide canine circles, a vast haze of auditory stuff
with every dog augmenting it, tail up, mouth serrated, shoulder ruff
pulsing with its outputs, a continuous clipped yap from a handmuff
Pomeranian, a labrador's ascending fours, a Dane grown great enough
to bark in the singular, many raffish bitzers blowing their gaff
as humans raise windows and cries and here and there the roof
and you barking at the epicentre, you, putting a warp to the woof,
shift the design with a throat-rubbing lull and ill howl,
dingo-vibrant, not shrill, which starts a howling school
among hill-and-hollow barkers, till horizons-wide again a tall
pavilion of mixed timbres is lifted up eerily in full call
and the wailing takes a toll: you, from playing the fool
move, behind your arch will, into the sorrow of a people.

— o —

And not just one people. You've entered a sound-proletariat
where pigs exclaim *boff-boff!* making off in fright
and fowls say *chirk* in tiny voices when a snake's about,
quite unlike the rooster's *Chook Chook*, meaning look, a good bit:
hens, get stoock into it! Where the urgent boar mutters *root-root*
to his small harassed sow, trotting back and forth beside her, *rut-rut*
and the she-cat's curdling *Mao?* where are kittens? mutating to *prr-mao*,
come along, kittens, are quite different words from *prr-au*,
general-welcome-and-acceptance, or extremity's portmanteau *mee-EU!*
Active and passive at once, the boar and feeding sow
share a common prone *unh*, expressing repletion and bestowing it,
and you're where the staid dog, excited, emits a mouth-skirl
he was trying to control, and looks ashamed of it
and the hawk above the land calls himself Peter P. P. Pew,
where, far from class hatred, the rooster scratches up some for you
and edgy plovers sharpen their nerves on a blurring wheel.
Waterbirds address you in their neck-flexure language, hiss and bow
and you speak to each species in the seven or eight
planetary words of its language, which ignore and include the detail

God set you to elaborate by the dictionary-full
when, because they would reveal their every secret,
He took definition from the beasts and gave it to you.

      — O —

If at baying time you have bayed with dogs and not humans
you know enough not to scorn the moister dimensions
of language, nor to build on the sandbanks of Dry.
You long to show someone non-human the diaphragm-shuffle
which may be your species' only distinctive cry,
the spasm which, in various rhythms, turns our face awry,
contorts speech, shakes the body, and makes our eyelids liquefy.
Approaching adulthood, one half of this makes us shy
and the other's a touchy spear-haft we wield for balance.
Laughter-and-weeping. It's the great term the small terms qualify
as a whale is qualified by all the near glitters of the sea.
Weightless leviathan our showering words overlie and modify,
it rises irresistibly. All our dry-eyed investigations
supply that one term, in the end; its occasions multiply,
the logics issue in horror, we are shattered by joy
till the old prime divider bends and its two ends unify
and the learned words bubble off us. We laugh because we cry:
the crying depth of life is too great not to laugh
but laugh or cry singly aren't it: only mingled are they spirit
to wobble and sing us as a summer dawn sings a magpie.
For spirit is the round earth bringing our flat earths to bay
and we're feasted and mortified, exposed to those momentary heavens
which, speaking in speech on the level, we work for and deny.

Time Travel

To revisit the spitfire world
of the duel, you put on a suit
of white body armour, a helmet
like an insect's composite eye
and step out like a space walker
under haloed lights, trailing a cord.

Descending, with nodding foil in hand
towards the pomander-and-cravat sphere
you meet the Opponent, for this journey
can only be accomplished by a pair
who semaphore and swap quick respect
before they set about their joint effect

which is making zeroes and serifs so
swiftly and with such sprung variety
that the long steels skid, clatter, zing,
switch, batter, bite, kiss and ring
in the complex rhythms of that society
with its warrior snare of comme il faut

that has you facing a starched beau
near stable walls on a misty morning,
striking, seeking the surrender in him,
the pedigree-flaw through which to pin him,
he probing for your own braggadocio,
confusion, ennui or inner fawning —

Seconds, holding stakes and cloths, look grim
and surge a step. Exchanges halt
for one of you stands, ageing horribly,
collapses, drowning from an entry
of narrow hurt. The other gulps hot chocolate
a trifle fast, but talking nonchalant —

a buzzer sounds. Heads are tucked
under arms, and you and he swap
curt nods in a more Christian century.

Exile Prolonged by Real Reasons

I have no right to what I need
The flying fox crawls on the ground

My father driving fast at seventeen
in a blue Dodge with spoked dog-killing wheels

winds north through the sandstone plateau country
its bared contour lines, its oyster rivers

its pastry-flour soil, its rusting creeks
he sees it as country not fit to farm

so send her for the long split rails of home
thirty years till he'd drive that road again

but the Blue Flyer dwindles ahead of dust
I drive back from life on a Sunday afternoon

When the flying fox first hit the ground
the road signs that point where my pain homed

all used to say eight: now they said thirteen
I brought the Gloucester road to mind

every cutting and bank on those twenty-five miles:
which was grassy, which gravel, which grew wild vines

Now the Blue Flyer's driver grows old all alone
I have no right to help his need

Between sitting like Jacky at boarding house meals
tram bells, and waterfalls loosed with a chain

my father in Sydney on that trip
rocked over the Harbour on a drenched ship

his mentor Jock Affleck wished bound for Home
storms and all. Jock never saw Scotland again

I haunted Central Station in my turn
to hear names, or a suitcase called a port

this even as I was learning to judge landscape
not for food, but blasphemously, as landscape

A world of understanding for a world of interest
I prised that trap open each time it went Swap

that isn't the wire that brought the fox down
I have no right to what I need.

Three Interiors

The mansard roof of the Barrier Industrial Council's
pale-blue Second Empire building in Broken Hill
announces the form of a sprightly, intricately painted
pressed metal ceiling, spaciously stepped and tie-beamed
high over the main meeting hall. The factual light
of the vast room is altered, in its dusty rising
toward that coloured mime of myriadness, that figured
carpet of the mind, whose marvel comes down the clean walls
almost to the shoulder-stain level, the rubbings of mass defiance
which circle the hall miner-high above worn-out timber flooring.
Beauty all suspended in air — I write from memory
but it was so when we were there. A consistent splendour,
quite abstract, bloc-voted, crystalline with colour junctions
and regulated tendrils, high in its applied symphonic theory
above the projection hatch, over sports gear and the odd steel chair
marooned on the splintery extents of the former dance floor.

The softly vaulted ceiling of St Gallen's monastic library
is beautifully iced in Rococo butter cream with scrolled pipework
surf-dense around islands holding russet-clad, vaguely heavenly
personages who've swum up from the serried volumes below.
The books themselves, that vertical live leather brickwork
in the violin-curved, gleaming bays, have all turned their backs
on the casual tourist and, clasped in meditation, they pray
in coined Greek, canonical Latin, pointed Hebrew.
It is an utterly quiet pre-industrial machine room
on a submarine to Heaven, and the deck, the famous floor
over which you pad in blanket slippers, has flowed in
honey-lucent around the footings, settled suavely level and hardened:
only the winding darker woods and underwater star-points
of the parquetry belie that impression. What is below
resembles what's above, but just enough, as cloud-shadow,
runways and old lake shores half noticed in mellow wheat land.

The last interior is darkness. Befuddled past-midnight
fear, testing each step like deep water, that when you open
the eventual refrigerator, cold but no light will envelop you.
Bony hurts that persuade you the names of your guides now
are balance, and gravity. You can fall up things, but not far.
A stopping, teeming caution. As of prey. The dark is arbitrary
delivering wheeled smashes, murmurings, something that scuttled,
doorjambs without a switch. The dark has no subject matter
but is alive with theory. Its best respites are: no surprises.
Nothing touching you. Or panic-stilling chance embraces.
Darkness is the cloth for pained eyes, and lovely in colour,

splendid in the lungs of great singers. Also the needed matrix
of constellations, flaring Ginzas, desert moons, apparent snow,
veranda-edged night rain. Dark is like that: all productions.
Almost nothing there is caused, or has results. Dark is all one interior
permitting only inner life. Concealing what will seize it.

Morse

Tuckett. Bill Tuckett. Telegraph operator, Hall's Creek
which is way out back of the Outback, but he stuck it,
quite likely liked it, despite heat, glare, dust and the lack
of diversion or doctors. Come disaster you trusted to luck,
ingenuity and pluck. This was back when nice people said pluck,
the sleevelink and green eyeshade epoch.
                         Faced, though, like Bill Tuckett
with a man needing surgery right on the spot, a lot
would have done their dashes. It looked hopeless (dot dot dot)
Lift him up on the table, said Tuckett, running the key hot
till Head Office turned up a doctor who coolly instructed
up a thousand miles of wire, as Tuckett advanced slit by slit
with a safety razor blade, pioneering on into the wet,
copper-wiring the rivers off, in the first operation conducted
along dotted lines, with rum drinkers gripping the patient:
d-d-dash it, take care, Tuck!
                      And the vital spark stayed unshorted.
Yallah! breathed the camelmen. Tuckett, you did it, you did it!
cried the spattered la-de-dah jodhpur-wearing Inspector of Stock.
We imagine, some weeks later, a properly laconic
convalescent averring Without you, I'd have kicked the bucket...

From Chungking to Burrenjuck, morse keys have mostly gone silent
and only old men meet now to chit-chat in their electric
bygone dialect. The last letter many will forget
is dit-dit-dit-dah, V for Victory. The coders' hero had speed,
resource and a touch. So ditditdit daah for Bill Tuckett.

Late Snow in Edinburgh

Snow on the day before Anzac!
A lamb-killing wind out of Ayr
heaped a cloud up on towering Edinburgh
in the night, and left it adhering
to parks and leafing trees in the morning,
a cloud decaying on the upper city,
on the stepped medieval skyscrapers there,
cassata broadcast on the lower city
to be a hiss on buzzing cobblestones
under soaped cars, and cars still shaving.

All day the multiplying whiteness
persisted, now dazzling, now resumed
into the spectral Northern weather,
moist curd out along the Castle clifftops,
linen collar on the Mound, pristine pickings
in the Cowgate's blackened teeth, deposits
in Sir Walter Scott's worked tusk, and under
the soaked blue banners walling Princes Street.
The lunchtime gun fired across dun distances
ragged with keen tents. By afternoon, though,
derelicts sleeping immaculate in wynds
and black areas had shrivelled to wet sheep.
Froth, fading, stretched thinner on allotments.

As the melting air browned into evening
the photographed city, in last umber
and misty first lights, was turning into
the stones in a vast furrow. For that moment
half a million moved in an earth cloud
harrowed up, damp and fuming, seeded
with starry points, with luminous still patches
that wouldn't last the night. No Anzac Day
prodigies for the visitor-descendant.
The snow was dimming into Spring's old
Flanders jacket and frieze trousers. Hughie Spring,
the droll ploughman, up from the Borders.

Art History: The Suburb of Surrealls

We dreamed very wide awake
those days, for obedience's sake:

*In the suburb of Surrealls
horse families board the airline bus
to sell packages of phlegm.
My notebook is hugely swollen.
For some reason I am American.*

Such dreaming is enforceable.
Everyone became guarded;
a tinkling of symbols was heard.
It's the West occupying the dreamworld
because the East has captured reason,
some said. Many ceased to listen.

In fact we'd gone to the dream
for supplies of that instant
paint of the twilight kingdom
which colours every object
supernal, deeply important.
Spirit-surrogate. We even synthesised it.

Exposed to the common air, it
weathered quickly to the tone
of affectless weird despair,
elegant barely contained anger
our new patrons demanded
when we had trained them to it.

False dreamings are imperial
but we couldn't disappoint them
(Few others now read us by choice.
Woolf! Woolf! our master's voice).

To be fair, many of us
had now joined the creative class
and become our masters
— but the paint, when stolen
and breathed straight from the tin
gave a noble deathly rush
that ensnared imagination.

The Dialectic of Dreams

Dream harbours Sin, and Innocence, and Magic,
re-stews mundane cabbage, stacks a shifting Tarot,
equivocates naively about Death, the secular Absolute —

things Rationality, the replacement aristocrat
approves only for enhancement. By midday
it has clarified its twinship with that relic —

but comes round again, by night at the latest,
in a skin boat sailing on the blood
for dream lives its life engorged. It owns tumescence,

makes eerie conquests, can engender children —
though few who see the sun. The real takes some joint permission:
two in one, ideally twice, before one and one

make One, Three, a Third, or two as one,
all those numbers of the dream mathematic.

— O —

Real dreams are from home • back there. The light as it was,
will be, might have been • all the receding dream-tenses.

The dreamer is even yourself • or you're aware it is.
There in the action, unsafe • greater than the action, passive,

rarely uttering, in the endless • preparations, for horror, for happiness,
those appalling formulae • other-directed at us

which may persist as salt foam • on the margin of lapsed scenes
or, like the filmed cities, be resumed • into their own presence.

And that otherworld near-compliance • spindling faintly through the day,
heightening thought, blanking it • silvering, beckoning away:

preternatural, those interiors • half-recalled by consciousness,
they were never in this world • nor in your life, those wet bossed lanes.

Yet this is the heart of work • *the human sage, the butterfly*
to be conscious at the source of worlds • rapt, raising the ante.

— O —

The daylight oil, the heavier grade of Reason,
reverie's clear water, that of the dreamworld ocean
agitate us and are shaken, forming the emulsion

without which we make nothing much. Not art,
not love, not war, nor its reasoned nightmare methods,
not the Taj, not our homes, not the Masses or the gods

— but the fusion persists in the product, not in us.
A wheel shatters, drains our pooled rainbow. It was a moment:
the world is debris and museum of that moment,

its prospectus and farm. The wheel is turned by this engine.
I think of the people and buildings in a business street,
how they lack a perfect valve to take on and release

successive visions. And will be pulled down for it,
their walls dreamed on in the milk of obsolete children.

      — O —

Dream surrounds, is infused with this world. It is not subordinate.
We come from it; we live at tangents and accords with it; we go
back into it, at last, through the drowsing torture chambers to it.

We have gills for dream-life, in our head; we must keep them wet
from the nine-nights' immense, or dreams will emerge bodily, and enforce it.
Hide among or deny the shallow dreadful ones, and they may stay out:

moor things in Heaven and earth then, Ratio, anyhow you can
because dream's the looseleaf book, not of fiction, but of raw Pretend,
incalculable as this world when the God of Mercy intervened often.

It is the free splitting from God that parts Nature from dream.
They refresh each other with bafflement, each as the other's underground
freeing lives to be finite, because more; to be timeless, yet pure preparation —

while those spaces, sacred as the poor, of the haloed russet kingdom
are tigers impelling us, full of futures and pasts, toward the present.

Satis Passio

Elites, levels, proletariat:
the uniting cloth crowns
of Upper and Lower Egypt
suggest theories of poetry
which kindness would accept
to bestow, like Heaven, dignity
on the inept and the ept,
one Papuan warrior's phallocrypt
the soaring equal of its fellowcrypt.

By these measures, most knowledge
in our heads is poetry,
varied crystals of detail, chosen
by dream-interest, and poured spirally
from version to myth, with spillage,
from theory to history
and, with toppings-up, to story,
not metered, lined or free
but condensed by memory
to roughly vivid essences:
most people's poetry is now this.
Some of it is made by poets.

God bless the feral poetries,
littératures and sensibilities,
theory, wonder, the human gamut
leaping cheerfully or in heavy earnest
— but there is this quality to art
which starts, rather than ends, at the gist.
Not the angle, but the angel.

Art is what can't be summarised:
it has joined creation from our side,
entered Nature, become a fact
and acquired presence,
more like ourselves or any subject
swirled around, about, in and out,
than like the swirling poetries.

Art's best is a standing miracle
at an uncrossable slight distance,
an anomaly, finite but inexhaustible,
unaltered after analysis
as an ancient face.

Not the portrait of one gone
merely, no pathos of the bygone
but a section, of all that exist,
a passage, a whole pattern
that has shifted the immeasurable
first step into Heaven.
A first approximation.
Where is Heaven? Down these roads.

The fine movement of art's face
before us is a motionless traffic
between here and remote Heaven.
It is out through this surface,
we may call it the Unfalling Arrow,
this third mode, and perhaps by art first
that there came to us the dream-plan
of equality and justice,
long delayed by the poetries —

but who was the more numinous,
Pharaoh or the hunted Nile heron?
more splendid, the iris or Solomon?
Beauty lives easily with equities
more terrible than theory dares mean.
Of the workers set free to break stone
and the new-cracked stone, which is more luminous?

God bless the general poetries?
This is how it's done.